SPANISH-ENGLISH
Picture Dictionary

Catherine Bruzzone and Louise Millar

Illustrations by Louise Comfort and Steph Dix
Spanish adviser: Diego Blasco Vázquez

B.E.S.
PUBLISHING

1 one
uno/una
OO-noh/OO-nah

2 two
dos
dohs

3 three
tres
trehs

4 four
cuatro
KWAH-troh

5 five
cinco
SEEN-koh

6 six
seis
sayss

7 seven
siete
see-EH-teh

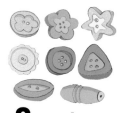

8 eight
ocho
OH-choh

9 nine
nueve
noo-EH-veh

10 ten
diez
dee-EHS

11
eleven
once
ON-seh

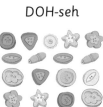

12
twelve
doce
DOH-seh

13
thirteen
trece
TREH-seh

14
fourteen
catorce
kah-TOHR-seh

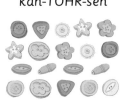

15
fifteen
quince
KEEN-seh

16
sixteen
dieciséis
dee-eh-see-SAYSS

17
seventeen
diecisiete
dee-eh-see-see-EH-teh

18
eighteen
dieciocho
dee-eh-see-OH-choh

19
nineteen
diecinueve
dee-eh-see-noo-EH-veh

20
twenty
veinte
VEH-een-teh

Contents – Índice

EEN-dee-seh

The body – El cuerpo
ehl koo-EHR-poh

head
la cabeza
lah kah-BEH-sah

eyes
los ojos
lohs OH-hos

nose
la nariz
lah nah-REES

mouth
la boca
lah BOH-kah

shoulders
los hombros
lohs OHM-brohs

arm
el brazo
ehl BRAH-soh

hand
la mano
lah MAH-noh

leg
la pierna
lah pee-EHR-nah

foot
el pie
ehl pee-EH

Clothes – La ropa
lah ROH-pah

skirt
la falda
lah FAHL-dah

dress
el vestido
ehl vehs-TEE-doh

pants
el pantalón
ehl pahn-tah-LOHN

coat
el abrigo
ehl ah-BREE-goh

shirt
la camisa
lah kah-MEE-sah

pajamas
el pijama
ehl pee-HAH-mah

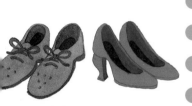

shoes
los zapatos
lohs sah-PAH-tohs

socks
los calcetines
lohs kahl-see-TEE-nehs

hat
el sombrero
ehl sohm-BREH-roh

5

The family – La familia
lah fah-MEE-lee-ah

mother/Mom
la madre/mamá
lah MAH-dreh/mah-MAH

father/Dad
el padre/papá
ehl PAH-dreh/pah-PAH

sister
la hermana
lah ehr-MAH-nah

brother
el hermano
ehl ehr-MAH-noh

grandmother
la abuela
lah ah-BWEH-lah

grandfather
el abuelo
ehl ah-BWEH-loh

aunt
la tía
lah TEE-ah

uncle
el tío
ehl TEE-oh

cousins
los primos
lohs PREE-mohs

The house – La casa
lah KAH-sah

kitchen
la cocina
lah koh-SEE-nah

living room
el salón
ehl sah-LOHN

bedroom
el dormitorio
ehl-dohr-mee-TOH-ree-oh

bathroom
l cuarto de baño
KWAHR-toh deh BAHN-yoh

toilet
el retrete
ehl reh-TREH-teh

stairs
las escaleras
lahs ehs-kah-LEH-rahs

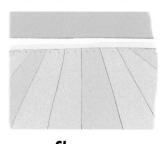

floor
el piso
ehl PEE-soh

ceiling
el techo
ehl TEH-choh

garden
el jardín
ehl hahr-DEEN

In the house – En la casa
ehn lah KAH-sah

sofa
el sofá
ehl soh-FAH

armchair
el sillón
ehl see-YOHN

cushion
el cojín
ehl koh-HEEN

curtains
las cortinas
lahs kohr-TEE-nahs

picture
el cuadro
ehl KWAH-droh

stool
el taburete
ehl tah-boo-REH-teh

telephone
el teléfono
ehl teh-LEH-foh-noh

computer
la computadora
lah kohm-poo-tah-DOH-rah

television
el televisor
ehl teh-leh-vee-SOHR

The kitchen – La cocina
lah koh-SEE-nah

sink
el fregadero
ehl freh-gah-DEH-roh

refrigerator
el refrigerador
ehl reh-free-heh-rah-DOHR

stove
la cocina
lah koh-SEE-nah

knife
el cuchillo
ehl koo-CHEE-yoh

spoon
la cuchara
lah koo-CHAH-rah

fork
el tenedor
ehl teh-neh-DOHR

plate
el plato
ehl PLAH-toh

glass
el vaso
ehl VAH-soh

pot
la cacerola
lah kah-seh-ROH-lah

9

The bedroom – El dormitorio

ehl dohr-mee-TOH-ree-oh

bed
la cama
lah KAH-mah

chest of drawers
la cómoda
lah KOH-moh-dah

wardrobe
el armario
ehl ahr-MAH-ree-oh

alarm clock
el despertador
ehl dehs-pehr-tah-DOHR

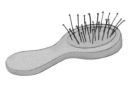

hairbrush
el cepillo del pelo
ehl seh-PEE-yoh dehl PEH-loh

shelf
el estante
ehl ehs-TAHN-teh

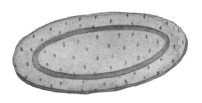

rug
la alfombra

lah ahl-FOHM-brah

window
la ventana
lah vehn-TAH-nah

door
la puerta
lah PWEHR-tah

washbowl
el lavamanos
ehl lah-vah-MAH-nohs

toilet
el retrete
ehl reh-TREH-teh

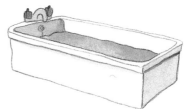

bathtub
la bañera
lah bahn-YEH-rah

shower
la ducha
lah DOO-chah

mirror
el espejo
ehl ehs-PEH-hoh

towel
la toalla
lah toh-AH-yah

toothpaste
pasta de dientes
PAHS-tah deh dee-EHN-tehs

toothbrush
el cepillo de dientes
ehl seh-PEE-yoh deh ee-EHN-tehs

soap
el jabón
ehl hah-BOHN

11

The city – La ciudad
lah see-oo-DAHD

house
la casa
lah KAH-sah

school
la escuela
lah ehs-KWEH-lah

station
la estación
lah ehs-tah-see-OHN

shop
la tienda
lah tee-EHN-dah

post office
la oficina de correos
lah oh-fee-SEE-nah deh
kohr-REH-ohs

supermarket
el supermercado
ehl soo-pehr-mehr-KAH-doh

factory
la fábrica
lah FAH-bree-kah

market
el mercado
ehl mehr-KAH-doh

cinema
el cine
ehl SEE-neh

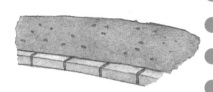

street
la calle
lah KAH-yeh

sidewalk
la acera
lah ah-SEH-rah

bus stop
la parada
lah pah-RAH-dah

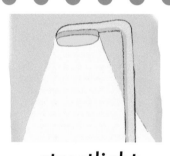

traffic light
el semáforo
ehl seh-MAH-foh-roh

roundabout
la rotonda
lah roh-TOHN-dah

streetlight
la farola
lah fah-ROH-lah

road sign
la señal de tráfico
sehn-YAHL deh TRAH-fee-koh

zebra crossing
el paso de cebra
ehl PAH-soh deh SEH-brah

police officer
el policía
ehl poh-lee-SEE-ah   **13**

Vehicles – Los vehículos
lohs veh-EE-koo-lohs

bus
el autobús
ehl aw-toh-BOOS

ambulance
la ambulancia
lah ahm-boo-LAHN-see-ah

bicycle
la bicicleta
lah bee-see-KLEH-tah

car
el coche
ehl KOH-cheh

police car
el coche de policía
ehl KOH-cheh deh poh-lee-SEE-ah

motorcycle
la motocicleta
lah moh-toh-see-KLEH-ta

truck
el camión
ehl kah-mee-OHN

fire engine
el camión de bomberos
ehl kah-mee-OHN deh bohm-BEH-rohs

van
la furgoneta
lah foor-goh-NEH-tah

path
el camino
ehl kah-MEE-noh

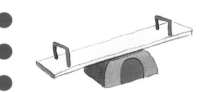

seesaw
el balancín
ehl bah-lahn-SEEN

swing
el columpio
ehl koh-LOOM-pee-oh

girl
la niña
lah NEEN-yah

boy
el niño
ehl NEEN-yoh

child
el niño/la niña
ehl NEEN-yoh/lah NEEN-yah

lake
el lago
ehl LAH-goh

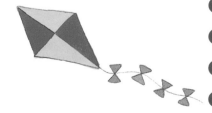

kite
la cometa
lah koh-MEH-tah

bench
el banco
ehl BAHN-koh

15

The hospital – El hospital

doctor
la doctora
lah dohk-TOH-rah

nurse
el enfermero
ehl ehn-fehr-MEH-roh

x-ray
la radiografía
lah rah-dee-oh-grah-FEE-a

thermometer
el termómetro
ehl tehr-MOH-meh-troh

medicine
la medicina
lah meh-dee-SEE-nah

bandage
el vendaje
ehl vehn-DAH-heh

cast
la escayola
lah ehs-kah-YOH-lah

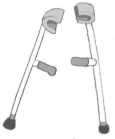

crutches
las muletas
lahs moo-LEH-tahs

wheelchair
la silla de rueda
lah SEE-yah deh RWEH-da

The supermarket – El supermercado

ehl soo-pehr-mehr-KAH-doh

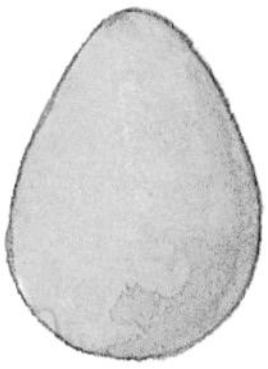

egg
el huevo
ehl HWEH-voh

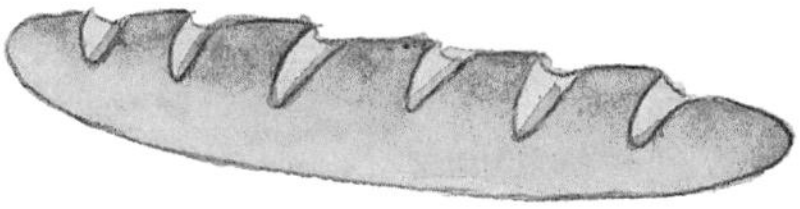

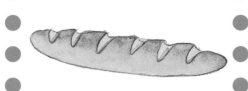

bread
el pan
ehl pahn

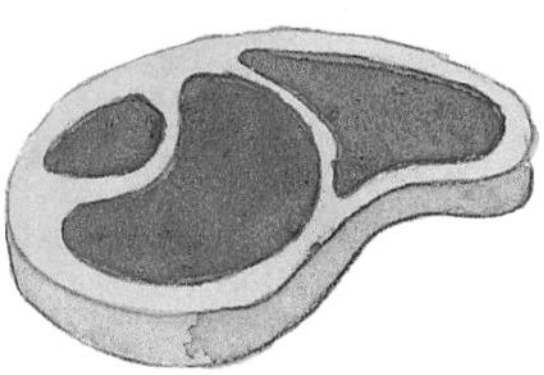

meat
la carne
lah KAHR-neh

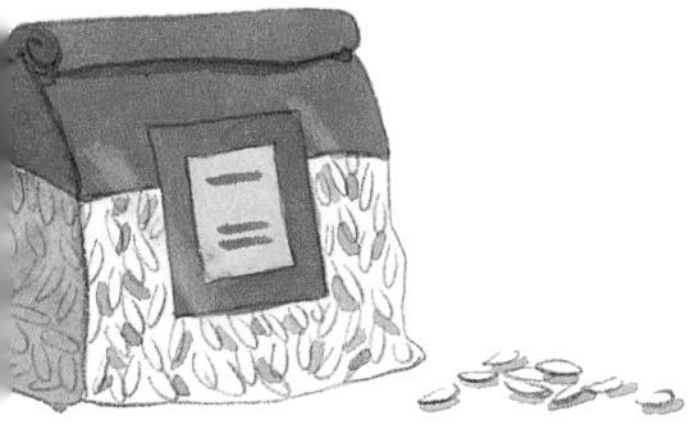

rice
el arroz
ehl ahr-ROHS

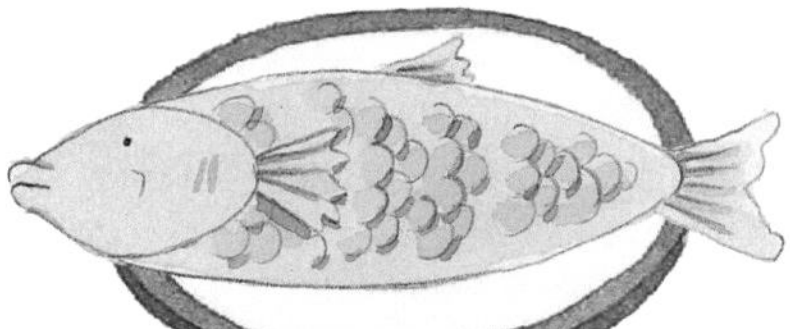

fish
el pescado
ehl pehs-KAH-doh

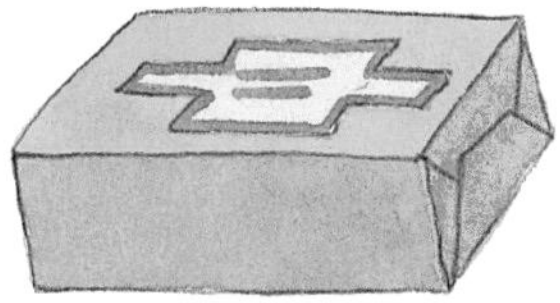

butter
la mantequilla
lah mahn-teh-KEE-yah

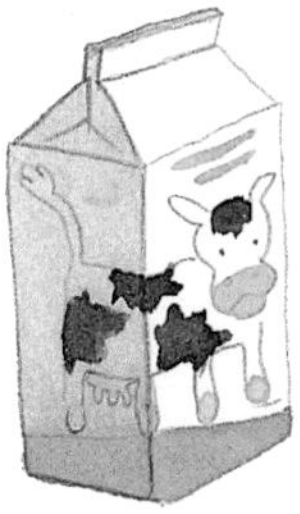

milk
la leche
lah LEH-cheh

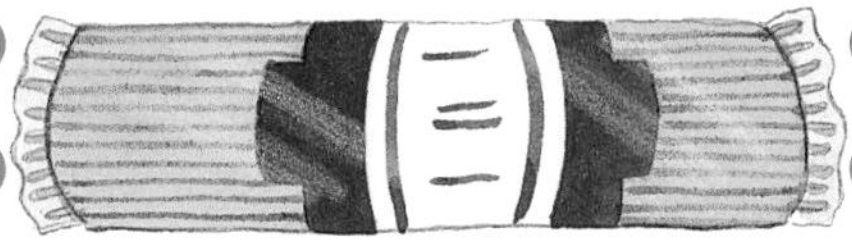

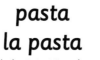

pasta
la pasta
lah PAHS-tah

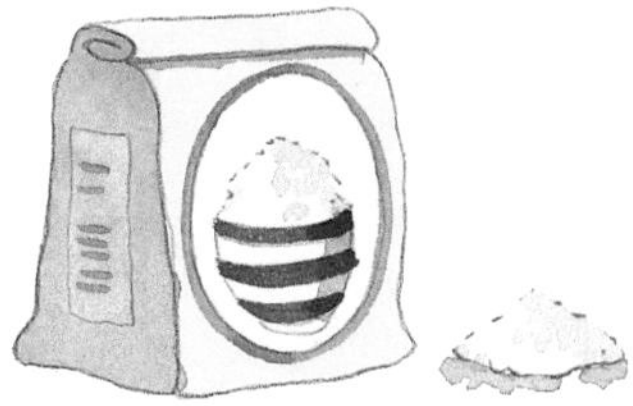

sugar
el azúcar
ehl ah-SOO-kahr

Fruit – La fruta
lah FROO-tah

apple
la manzana

lah mahn-SAH-nah

peach
el melocotón

ehl meh-loh-koh-TOHN

cherry
la cereza

lah seh-REH-sah

orange
la naranja

lah nah-RAHN-hah

pineapple
la piña

lah PEEN-yah

mango
el mango

ehl MAHN-goh

banana
el plátano

18 ehl PLAH-tah-noh

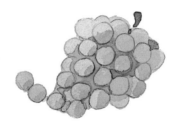

grapes
las uvas

lahs OO-vahs

strawberry
la fresa

lah FREH-sah

Vegetables – Las verduras

lahs vehr-DOO-rahs

potato
la papa
lah PAH-pah

corn
el maíz
ehl mah-EES

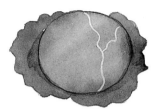

cabbage
la col
lah kohl

zucchini
el calabacín
ehl kah-lah-bah-SEEN

carrot
la zanahoria
lah sah-nah-OH-ree-ah

eggplant
la berenjena
lah beh-rehn-HEH-nah

tomato
el tomate
ehl toh-MAH-teh

lettuce
la lechuga
lah leh-CHOO-gah

celery
el apio
ehl AH-pee-oh

19

The country- El campo

ehl KAHM-poh

tree
el árbol
ehl AHR-bohl

grass
la hierba
lah ee-EHR-bah

flower
la flor
lah flohr

field
el prado
ehl PRAH-doh

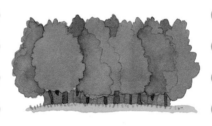

forest
el bosque
ehl BOHS-keh

mountain
la montaña
lah mohn-TAHN-yah

bridge
el puente
ehl PWEHN-teh

river
el río
ehl REE-oh

bird
el pájaro
ehl PAH-hah-roh

In the forest – En el bosque

fox
el zorro
ehl SOHR-roh

squirrel
la ardilla
lah ahr-DEE-yah

deer
el ciervo
ehl see-EHR-voh

rabbit
el conejo
ehl koh-NEH-hoh

brown bear
el oso marrón
ehl OH-soh mahr-ROHN

butterfly
la mariposa
lah mah-ree-POH-sah

beetle
el escarabajo
ehl ehs-kah-rah-BAH-hoh

caterpillar
la oruga
lah oh-ROO-gah

fly
la mosca
lah MOHS-kah

21

The farm – La granja
lah GRAHN-hah

cat
el gato
ehl GAH-toh

mouse
el ratón
ehl rah-TOHN

dog
el perro
ehl PEHR-roh

cow
la vaca
lah VAH-kah

horse
el caballo
ehl kah-BAH-yoh

pig
el cerdo
ehl SEHR-doh

sheep
la oveja
lah oh-VEH-hah

duck
el pato
ehl PAH-toh

goat
la cabra
lah KAH-brah

lahs KREE-ahs deh ah-nee-MAH-lehs

puppy
el cachorro
ehl kah-CHOHR-roh

kitten
el gatito
ehl gah-TEE-toh

foal
el potro
ehl POH-troh

calf
el ternero
ehl tehr-NEH-roh

chick
el pollito
ehl poh-YEE-toh

cygnet
el pichón de cisne
ehl pee-CHOHN deh SEES-neh

duckling
el patito
ehl pah-TEE-toh

lamb
el cordero
ehl kohr-DEH-roh

piglet
el cerdito
ehl sehr-DEE-toh

23

At the beach – En la playa
ehn lah PLAH-yah

sea
el mar
ehl mahr

seagull
la gaviota
lah gah-vee-OH-tah

sand
la arena
lah ah-REH-nah

fish
el pez
ehl pehs

seaweed
el alga marina
ehl AHL-gah mah-REE-nah

shell
la concha
lah KOHN-chah

rock
la roca
lah ROH-kah

sailboat
el velero
ehl veh-LEH-roh

wave
la ola
lah OH-lah

Under the sea – Bajo el mar

octopus
el pulpo
ehl POOL-poh

starfish
la estrella de mar
lah ehs-TREH-yah deh mahr

jellyfish
la medusa
lah meh-DOO-sah

lobster
la langosta
lah lahn-GOHS-tah

shark
el tiburón
ehl tee-boo-ROHN

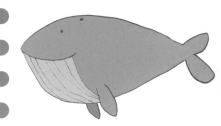

whale
la ballena
lah bah-YEH-nah

wreck
el naufragio
ehl nah-oo-FRAH-hee-oh

diver
el buceador
ehl boo-seh-ah-DOHR

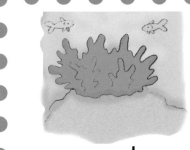

coral
el coral
ehl koh-RAHL

The zoo – El zoológico

giraffe
la jirafa

lah hee-RAH-fah

snake
la serpiente

lah sehr-pee-EHN-teh

hippopotamus
el hipopótamo

ehl ee-poh-POH-tah-moh

dolphin
el delfín

ehl dehl-FEEN

tiger
el tigre

ehl TEE-greh

crocodile
el cocodrilo

ehl koh-koh-DREE-loh

polar bear
el oso polar

26 *ehl OH-soh poh-LAHR*

lion
el león

ehl leh-OHN

elephant
el elefante

ehl eh-leh-FAHN-teh

Toys – Los juguetes

los hoo-GEH-tehs

teddy bear
el osito

ehl oh-SEE-toh

robot
el robot

ehl roh-BOHT

ball
la pelota

lah peh-LOH-tah

puzzle
el rompecabezas

l rohm-peh-kah-BEH-sahs

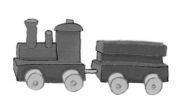

toy train
el trencito de juguete

ehl trehn-SEE-toh deh hoo-GEH-teh

game
el juego

ehl HWEH-goh

doll
la muñeca

lah moon-YEH-kah

paints
las pinturas

lahs peen-TOO-rahs

drum
el tambor

ehl tahm-BOHR

27

Party time! – ¡Fiesta!
fee-EHS-tah

sandwich
el bocadillo
ehl boh-kah-DEE-yoh

chocolate
el chocolate
ehl choh-koh-LAH-teh

french fries
las papas fritas
lahs PAH-pahs FREE-tahs

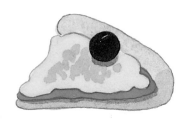

pizza
la pizza
lah PEE-tsah

cake
la torta
lah TOHR-tah

ice cream
el helado
ehl eh-LAH-doh

cola
el refresco
ehl reh-FREHS-koh

orange juice
el jugo de naranja
ehl HOO-goh deh nah-RAHN-hah

water
el agua
ehl AH-gwah

28

The classroom – La clase

lah KLAH-seh

teacher
la profesora

lah proh-feh-SOH-rah

table
la mesa

lah MEH-sah

chair
la silla

lah SEE-yah

book
el libro

ehl LEE-broh

color pencil
el lápiz de color

ehl LAH-pees deh koh-LOHR

glue
el pegamento

ehl peh-gah-MEHN-toh

paper
el papel

ehl pah-PEHL

pen
la pluma

lah PLOO-mah

scissors
las tijeras

lahs tee-HEH-rahs **29**

Sports - Los deportes

lohs deh-POHR-tehs

soccer
el fútbol
ehl FOOT-bohl

table tennis
el ping pong
ehl peeng pohng

skiing
el esquí
ehl ehs-KEY

gymnastics
la gimnasia
lah heem-NAH-see-ah

cycling
el ciclismo
ehl see-KLEES-moh

athletics
el atletismo
ehl aht-leh-TEES-moh

fishing
la pesca
lah PEHS-kah

swimming
la natación
lah nah-tah-see-OHN

basketball
el baloncesto
ehl bah-lohn-SEHS-toh

Weather – El tiempo

ehl tee-EHM-poh

sun
el sol
ehl sohl

heat
el calor
ehl kah-LOHR

rain
la lluvia
lah YOO-vee-ah

cloud
la nube
lah NOO-beh

wind
el viento
ehl vee-EHN-toh

storm
la tormenta
lah tohr-MEHN-tah

fog
la niebla
lah nee-EH-blah

cold
el frío
ehl FREE-oh

snow
la nieve
lah nee-EH-veh

Action words – Palabras de acción

pah-LAH-brahs deh ahk-see-OHN

to run
correr
kohr-REHR

to walk
andar
ahn-DAHR

to crawl
gatear
gah-teh-AHR

to carry
llevar
yeh-VAHR

to stand
estar de pie
ehs-TAHR deh pee-EH

to sit
estar sentado
ehs-TAHR sehn-TAH-doh

to push
empujar
ehm-poo-HAHR

to hug
abrazar
ah-brah-SAHR

to pull
halar
hah-LAHR

Storybooks – Los libros de cuentos

dragon
el dragón
ehl drah-GOHN

mermaid
la sirena
lah see-REH-nah

knight
el caballero
ehl kah-bah-YEH-roh

pirate
el pirata
ehl pee-RAH-tah

fairy
el hada
ehl AH-dah

witch
la bruja
lah BROO-hah

prince
el príncipe
ehl PREEN-see-peh

princess
la princesa
lah preen-SEH-sah

castle
el castillo
ehl kahs-TEE-yoh

33

The building site – La obra
lah OH-brah

digger
la excavadora
lah ex-kah-vah-DOH-rah

cement mixer
el camión hormigonera
ehl kah-mee-OHN
ohr-mee-goh-NEH-rah

crane
la grúa
lah GROO-ah

scaffolding
el andamio
ehl ahn-DAH-mee-oh

dump truck
el camión volquete
ehl kah-mee-OHN vohl-KEH-teh

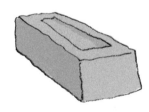

brick
el ladrillo
ehl lah-DREE-yoh

bulldozer
el bulldozer
ehl bool-DOH-zehr

ladder
la escalera
lah ehs-kah-LEH-rah

wood
el tablón
ehl tah-BLOHN

Tools – Las herramientas

rake
el rastrillo
ehl rahs-TREE-yoh

shovel
la pala
lah PAH-lah

bucket
el cubo
ehl KOO-boh

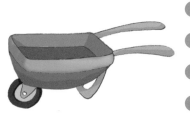

wheelbarrow
la carretilla
lah kahr-reh-TEE-yah

hammer
el martillo
ehl mahr-TEE-yoh

nail
el clavo
ehl KLAH-voh

saw
el serrucho
ehl sehr-ROO-choh

hose
la manguera
lah mahn-GEH-rah

paintbrush
la brocha
lah BROH-chah

35

Luggage – El equipaje
ehl eh-kee-PAH-heh

suitcase
la maleta
lah mah-LEH-tah

schoolbag
el bolsón
ehl bohl-SOHN

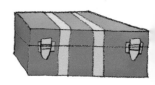

trunk
el baúl
ehl bah-OOL

backpack
la mochila
lah moh-CHEE-lah

handbag
la cartera
lah kahr-TEH-rah

briefcase
el maletín
ehl mah-leh-TEEN

basket
la cesta
lah SEHS-tah

shopping bag
la bolsa de compras
lah BOHL-sah deh KOHM-prahs

purse
el monedero
ehl moh-neh-DEH-roh

Train travel – El viaje en tren

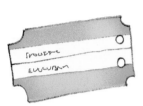

ticket
el billete

ehl bee-YEH-teh

conductor
el revisor

ehl reh-vee-SOHR

platform
el andén

ehl ahn-DEHN

engineer
la maquinista

lah mah-kee-NEES-tah

signal
la señal

lah sehn-YAHL

train
el tren

ehl trehn

seat
el asiento

ehl ah-see-EHN-toh

level crossing
el paso a nivel

ehl PAH-soh ah nee-VEHL

rails
los rieles

lohs ree-EH-lehs

37

Air travel – El viaje en avión

ehl vee-AH-heh ehn ah-vee-OHN

airplane
el avión

ehl ah-vee-OHN

airport
el aeropuerto

ehl ah-eh-roh-PWEHR-toh

pilot
el piloto

ehl pee-LOH-toh

flight attendant
la azafata

lah ah-sah-FAH-tah

x-ray machine
la máquina de rayos x

lah MAH-kee-nah
deh RAH-yohs EH-kees

passport
el pasaporte

ehl pah-sah-POHR-teh

hand truck
el carrito

ehl kahr-REE-toh

snack
el refrigerio

ehl reh-free-HEH-ree-oh

seatbelt
el cinturón de seguria

ehl seen-too-ROHN deh
seh-goo-ree-DAHD

At sea – En el mar

ehn ehl mahr

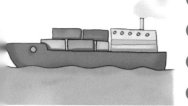

ship
el barco

ehl BAHR-koh

yacht
el yate

ehl YAH-teh

rowboat
el bote a remos

ehl BOH-teh ah REH-mohs

tanker
el petrolero

ehl peh-troh-LEH-roh

fishing boat
el barco de pesca

ehl BAHR-koh deh PEHS-kah

ferry
el ferry

ehl FEHR-ree

buoy
la boya

lay BOH-yah

port
el puerto

ehl PWEHR-toh

lighthouse
el faro

ehl FAH-roh

39

Opposites – Los contrarios
lohs kohn-TRAH-ree-ohs

friendly
amable
ah-MAH-bleh

angry
enojado/enojada
eh-noh-HAH-doh/eh-noh-HAH-dah

thin
delgado/delgad⟨
dehl-GAH-doh/dehl-GAH-d⟨

clean
limpio/limpia
LEEM-pee-oh/LEEM-pee-ah

dirty
sucio/sucia
SOO-see-oh/SOO-see-ah

neat
ordenado/ordena⟨
ohr-deh-NAH-doh/ohr-deh-NAH⟨

sad
triste
TREES-teh

40

happy
feliz
feh-LEES

heavy
pesado/pesada
peh-SAH-doh/peh-SAH-d⟨

Opposites – Los contrarios

fat
gordo/gorda
GOHR-doh/GOHR-dah

tall
alto/alta
AHL-toh/AHL-tah

short
bajo/baja
BAH-hoh/BAH-hah

messy
desordenado/desordenada
deh-sohr-deh-NAH-doh/
deh-sohr-deh-NAH-dah

fast
rápido/rápida
RAH-pee-doh/RAH-pee-dah

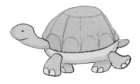

slow
lento/lenta
LEHN-toh/LEHN-tah

light
ligero/ligera
lee-HEH-roh/lee-HEH-rah

beautiful
hermoso/hermosa
ehr-MOH-soh/ehr-MOH-sah

ugly
feo/fea
FEH-oh/FEH-ah

41

Spanish/español – English/inglés

abrazar to hug
el abrigo coat
la abuela grandmother
el abuelo grandfather
la acera sidewalk
el aeropuerto airport
el agua water
la alfombra rug
el alga marina seaweed
alto/alta tall
amable friendly
amarillo/amarilla yellow
la ambulancia ambulance
el andamio scaffolding
andar to walk
el andén platform
el apio celery
el árbol tree
la ardilla squirrel
la arena sand
el armario wardrobe
el arroz rice
el asiento seat
el atletismo athletics
el autobús bus
el avión airplane
la azafata flight attendant
el azúcar sugar
azul blue
bajo/baja short
el balancín seesaw
la ballena whale
el baloncesto basketball
el banco bench
la bañera bathtub
el barco ship
el barco de pesca fishing boat
el baúl trunk
la berenjena eggplant
la bicicleta bicycle
el billete ticket

blanco/blanca white
la boca mouth
el bocadillo sandwich
la bolsa de compras shopping bag
el bolsón schoolbag
el bosque forest
el bote a remos rowboat
la boya buoy
el brazo arm
la brocha paintbrush
la bruja witch
el buceador diver
el bulldozer bulldozer
el caballero knight
el caballo horse
la cabeza head
la cabra goat
la cacerola pot
el cachorro puppy
el calabacín zucchini
los calcetines socks
la calle street
el calor heat
la cama bed
el camino path
el camión truck
el camión de bomberos fire engine
el camión hormigonera
  cement mixer
el camión volquete dump truck
la camisa shirt
el campo country
la carne meat
la carretilla wheelbarrow
la cartera handbag
el carrito hand truck
la casa house
el castillo castle
catorce fourteen
el cepillo de dientes toothbrush
el cepillo del pelo hairbrush
el cerdito piglet

el cerdo pig
la cereza cherry
la cesta basket
el chocolate chocolate
el ciclismo cycling
el ciervo deer
cinco five
el cine cinema
el cinturón de seguridad seatbelt
la ciudad city
la clase classroom
el clavo nail
el coche car
el coche de policía police car
la cocina kitchen, stove
el cocodrilo crocodile
el cojín cushion
la col cabbage
los colores colors
la cometa kite
la cómoda chest of drawers
la computadora computer
la concha shell
el conejo rabbit
el coral coral
el cordero lamb
correr to run
las cortinas curtains
el cuadro picture
el cuarto de baño bathroom
cuatro four
el cubo bucket
la cuchara spoon
el cuchillo knife
el cuerpo body
el delfín dolphin
delgado/delgada thin
los deportes sports
desordenado/desordenada messy
el despertador alarm clock
diecinueve nineteen
dieciocho eighteen

42

...eciséis sixteen
...ecisiete seventeen
...ez ten
...ce twelve
...doctora doctor
...dormitorio bedroom
...s two
...dragón dragon
...ducha shower
...elefante elephant
...npujar to push
...enfermero nurse
...ojado/enojada angry
...equipaje luggage
...escalera ladder
...s escaleras stairs
...escarabajo beetle
...escayola cast
...escuela school
...espejo mirror
...esquí skiing
...estación station
...estante shelf
...tar de pie to stand
...tar sentado to sit
...estrella de mar starfish
...excavadora digger
...fábrica factory
...falda skirt
...familia family
...faro lighthouse
...farola streetlight
...liz happy
...o/fea ugly
...ferry ferry
...fiesta party
...flor flower
...fregadero sink
...fresa strawberry
...frío cold
...fruta fruit
...furgoneta van
...fútbol soccer
...atear to crawl
...gatito kitten

el gato cat
la gaviota seagull
la gimnasia gymnastics
gordo/gorda fat
la granja farm
la grúa crane
el hada fairy
halar to pull
el helado ice cream
la hermana sister
el hermano brother
hermoso/hermosa beautiful
las herramientas tools
la hierba grass
el hipopótamo hippopotamus
los hombros shoulders
el hospital hospital
el huevo egg
el jabón soap
el jardín garden
la jirafa giraffe
el jugo de naranja orange juice
el juguete toy
el ladrillo brick
el lago lake
la langosta lobster
el lápiz de color color pencil
el lavamanos washbowl
la leche milk
la lechuga lettuce
lento/lenta slow
el león lion
el libro book
ligero/ligera light
limpio/limpia clean
llevar to carry
la lluvia rain
la madre mother
el maíz corn
la maleta suitcase
el maletín briefcase
mamá Mom
el mango mango
la manguera hose
la mano hand

la mantequilla butter
la manzana apple
la máquina de rayos x x-ray machine
la maquinista engineer
el mar sea
la mariposa butterfly
marrón brown
el martillo hammer
la matación swimming
la medicina medicine
la medusa jellyfish
el melocotón peach
el mercado market
la mesa table
la mochila backpack
el monedero purse
la montaña mountain
morado/morada purple
la mosca fly
la motocicleta motorcycle
las muletas crutches
la muñeca doll
la naranja orange (fruit)
naranja orange (color)
la nariz nose
la natación swimming
el naufragio wreck
negro/negra black
la niebla fog
la nieve snow
la niña girl
el niño boy
el niño/la niña child
la nube cloud
nueve nine
la obra building site
ocho eight
la oficina de correos post office
los ojos eyes
la ola wave
once eleven
ordenado/ordenada neat
la oruga caterpillar
el osito teddy bear

el oso marrón brown bear
el oso polar polar bear
la oveja sheep
el padre father
el pájaro bird
la pala shovel
el pan bread
el pantalón pants
papá Dad
la papa potato
las papas fritas french fries
el papel paper
la parada bus stop
el pasaporte passport
el paso a nivel level crossing
el paso de cebra zebra crossing
la pasta pasta
la pasta de dientes toothpaste
el patito duckling
el pato duck
el pegamento glue
la pelota ball
el perro dog
pesado/pesada heavy
el pescado fish (to eat)
la pesca fishing
el petrolero tanker
el pez fish (in the sea)
el pichón de cisne cygnet
el pie foot
la pierna leg
el pijama pajamas
el piloto pilot
la piña pineapple
el ping pong table tennis
las pinturas paints
el pirata pirate
el piso floor
la pizza pizza
el plátano banana
el plato plate
la playa beach
la pluma pen
el policía police officer

el pollito chick
el potro foal
el prado field
los primos cousins
la princesa princess
el príncipe prince
la profesora teacher
el puente bridge
la puerta door
el puerto port
el pulpo octopus
quince fifteen
la radiografía x-ray
rápido/rápida fast
el rastrillo rake
el ratón mouse
el refresco cola
el refrigerador refrigerator
el refrigerio snack
el retrete toilet
el revisor conductor
los rieles rails
el río river
el robot robot
la roca rock
rojo/roja red
el rompecabezas puzzle
la ropa clothes
la rotonda roundabout
el salón living room
seis six
el semáforo traffic light
la señal signal
la señal de tráfico road sign
la serpiente snake
el serrucho saw
siete seven
la silla chair
la silla de ruedas wheelchair
el sillón armchair
la sirena mermaid
el sofá sofa
el sol sun
el sombrero hat
sucio/sucia dirty

el supermercado supermarket
el tablón wood
el taburete stool
el tambor drum
el techo ceiling
el teléfono telephone
el televisor television
el tenedor fork
el termómetro thermometer
el ternero calf
la tía aunt
el tiburón shark
el tiempo weather
la tienda shop
el tigre tiger
las tijeras scissors
el tío uncle
la toalla towel
el tomate tomato
la tormenta storm
la torta cake
trece thirteen
el tren train
el trencito de juguete toy train
tres three
triste sad
uno/una one
las uvas grapes
la vaca cow
el vaso glass
los vehículos vehicles
veinte twenty
el velero sailboat
el vendaje bandage
la ventana window
verde green
las verduras vegetables
el vestido dress
el viaje travel
el viento wind
el yate yacht
la zanahoria carrot
los zapatos shoes
el zoológico zoo
el zorro fox

English/inglés – Spanish/español

airplane el avión
airport el aeropuerto
alarm clock el despertador
ambulance la ambulancia
angry enojado/enojada
apple la manzana
arm el brazo
armchair el sillón
athletics el atletismo
aunt la tía
backpack la mochila
ball la pelota
banana el plátano
bandage el vendaje
basket la cesta
basketball el baloncesto
bathroom el cuarto de baño
bathtub la bañera
beach la playa
beautiful hermoso/hermosa
bed la cama
bedroom el dormitorio
beetle el escarabajo
bench el banco
bicycle la bicicleta
bird el pájaro
black negro/negra
blue azul
body el cuerpo
book el libro
boy el niño
bread el pan
brick el ladrillo
bridge el puente
briefcase el maletín
brother el hermano
brown marrón
brown bear el oso marrón
bucket el cubo
building site la obra
bulldozer el bulldozer
buoy la boya

bus el autobús
bus stop la parada
butter la mantequilla
butterfly la mariposa
cabbage la col
cake la torta
calf el ternero
car el coche
carrot la zanahoria
to carry llevar
cast la escayola
castle el castillo
cat el gato
caterpillar la oruga
ceiling el techo
celery el apio
cement mixer
  el camión hormigonera
chair la silla
cherry la cereza
chest of drawers la cómoda
chick el pollito
child el niño/la niña
chocolate el chocolate
cinema el cine
city la ciudad
classroom la clase
clean limpio/limpia
clothes la ropa
cloud la nube
coat el abrigo
cola el refresco
cold el frío
color pencil el lápiz de color
colors los colores
computer la computadora
conductor el revisor
coral el coral
corn el maíz
country el campo
cousins los primos
cow la vaca

crane la grúa
to crawl gatear
crocodile el cocodrilo
crutches las muletas
curtains las cortinas
cushion el cojín
cycling ciclismo
cygnet el pichón de cisne
Dad papá
deer el ciervo
digger la excavadora
dirty sucio/sucia
diver el buceador
doctor la doctora
dog el perro
doll la muñeca
dolphin el delfín
door la puerta
dragon el dragón
dress el vestido
drum el tambor
duck el pato
duckling el patito
dump truck el camión volquete
egg el huevo
eggplant la berenjena
eight ocho
eighteen dieciocho
elephant el elefante
eleven once
engineer la maquinista
eyes los ojos
factory la fábrica
fairy el hada
family la familia
farm la granja
fast rápido/rápida
fat gordo/gorda
father el padre
ferry el ferry
field el prado
fifteen quince

45

English	Spanish		English	Spanish		English	Spanish

fire engine el camión de bomberos
fish (to eat) el pescado
fish (in the sea) el pez
fishing la pesca
fishing boat el barco de pesca
five cinco
flight attendant la azafata
floor el piso
flower la flor
fly la mosca
foal el potro
fog la niebla
foot el pie
forest el bosque
fork el tenedor
four cuatro
fourteen catorce
fox el zorro
french fries las papas fritas
friendly amable
fruit la fruta
garden el jardín
giraffe la jirafa
girl la niña
glass el vaso
glue el pegamento
goat la cabra
grandfather el abuelo
grandmother la abuela
grapes las uvas
grass la hierba
green verde
gymnastics la gimnasia
hairbrush el cepillo del pelo
hammer el martillo
hand la mano
handbag la cartera
hand truck el carrito
happy feliz
hat el sombrero
head la cabeza
heat el calor
heavy pesado/pesada
hippopotamus el hipopótamo

horse el caballo
hose la manguera
hospital el hospital
house la casa
to hug abrazar
ice cream el helado
jellyfish la medusa
kitchen la cocina
kite la cometa
kitten el gatito
knife el cuchillo
knight el caballero
ladder la escalera
lake el lago
lamb el cordero
leg la pierna
lettuce la lechuga
level crossing el paso a nivel
light ligero/ligera
lighthouse el faro
lion el león
living room el salón
lobster la langosta
luggage el equipaje
mango el mango
market el mercado
meat la carne
medicine la medicina
mermaid la sirena
messy desordenado/desordenada
milk la leche
mirror el espejo
Mom mamá
mother la madre
motorcycle la motocicleta
mountain la montaña
mouse el ratón
mouth la boca
nail el clavo
neat ordenado/ordenada
nine nueve
nineteen diecinueve
nose la nariz
nurse el enfermero
octopus el pulpo

one uno/una
orange (fruit) la naranja
orange (color) naranja
orange juice el jugo de naranja
paintbrush la brocha
paints las pinturas
pajamas el pijama
pants el pantalón
paper el papel
party la fiesta
passport el pasaporte
pasta la pasta
path el camino
peach el melocotón
pen la pluma
picture el cuadro
pig el cerdo
piglet el cerdito
pilot el piloto
pineapple la piña
pirate el pirata
pizza la pizza
plate el plato
platform el andén
polar bear el oso polar
police car el coche de policía
police officer el policía
port el puerto
post office la oficina de correos
pot la cacerola
potato la papa
prince el príncipe
princess la princesa
to pull halar
puppy el cachorro
purple morado/morada
purse el monedero
to push empujar
puzzle el rompecabezas
rabbit el conejo
rails los rieles
rain la lluvia
rake el rastrillo
red rojo/roja
refrigerator el refrigerador

...ce el arroz	sixteen dieciséis	tomato el tomate
...ver el río	skiing el esquí	tools las herramientas
...ad sign la señal de tráfico	skirt la falda	toothbrush el cepillo de dientes
...bot el robot	slow lento/lenta	toothpaste la pasta de dientes
...ck la roca	snack el refrigerio	towel la toalla
...undabout la rotonda	snake la serpiente	toy el juguete
...wboat el bote a remos	snow la nieve	toy train el trencito de juguete
...g la alfombra	soap el jabón	traffic light el semáforo
run correr	soccer el fútbol	train el tren
...d triste	socks los calcetines	travel el viaje
...ilboat el velero	sofa el sofá	tree el árbol
...nd la arena	spoon la cuchara	truck el camión
...ndwich el bocadillo	sports los deportes	trunk el baúl
...w el serrucho	squirrel la ardilla	twelve doce
...affolding el andamio	stairs las escaleras	twenty veinte
...hool la escuela	to stand estar de pie	two dos
...hoolbag el bolsón	starfish la estrella de mar	ugly feo/fea
...issors las tijeras	station la estación	uncle el tío
...a el mar	stool el taburete	van la furgoneta
...agull la gaviota	storm la tormenta	vegetables las verduras
...at el asiento	stove la cocina	vehicles los vehículos
...atbelt el cinturón de seguridad	strawberry la fresa	to walk andar
...aweed el alga marina	street la calle	wardrobe el armario
...esaw el balancín	streetlight la farola	washbowl el lavabo
...ven siete	sugar el azúcar	water el agua
...venteen diecisiete	suitcase la maleta	wave la ola
...ark el tiburón	sun el sol	weather el tiempo
...eep la oveja	supermarket el supermercado	whale la ballena
...elf el estante	swimming la natación	wheelbarrow la carretilla
...ell la concha	table la mesa	wheelchair la silla de ruedas
...ip el barco	table tennis el ping pong	white blanco/blanca
...irt la camisa	tall alto/alta	wind el viento
...oes los zapatos	tanker el petrolero	window la ventana
...op la tienda	teacher la profesora	witch la bruja
...opping bag la bolsa de compras	teddy bear el osito	wood el tablón
...ort bajo/baja	telephone el teléfono	wreck el naufragio
...oulders los hombros	television el televisor	x-ray la radiografía
...ovel la pala	ten diez	x-ray machine
...hower la ducha	thermometer el termómetro	la máquina de rayos x
...dewalk la acera	thin delgado/delgada	yacht el yate
...gnal la señal	thirteen trece	yellow amarillo/amarilla
...ink el fregadero	three tres	zebra crossing el paso de cebra
...ister la hermana	ticket el billete	zoo el zoológico
...o sit estar sentado	tiger el tigre	zucchini el calabacín
...ix seis	toilet el retrete	

Colors – Los colores

red
rojo/roja
ROH-hoh/ROH-hah

blue
azul
ah-SOOL

green
verde
VEHR-deh

yellow
amarillo/amarilla
ah-mah-REE-yoh/
ah-mah-REE-yah

black
negro/negra
NEH-groh/NEH-grah

orange
naranja
nah-RAHN-hah

white
blanco/blanca
BLAHN-koh/BLAHN-kah

purple
morado/morada
moh-RAH-doh/moh-RAH-dah

brown
marrón
mahr-ROHN